Minimalism

This Is The Definitive Guide To Minimalism; Learn How To Declutter Your Home And Understand Why Less Is More; Enhance Your Quality Of Life By Adopting A Simple And Frugal Lifestyle

Mehmet Kunkel

TABLE OF CONTNET

Deliver A Safer Driving Experience. 1

Why Reduce? 10

The Whole Advantages Of Living A Minimalist Lifestyle..19

It Doesn't Have To Cost More To Be Minimalist 33

Acquiring The Viewpoint Of A Minimalist..................49

Restricting Options And Remedies................................75

Continue To Clear Your Clutter 98

Reduced-Total Productivity 115

A Well-Grounded Method...132

Deliver A Safer Driving Experience.

Minimalism has several benefits for your car. If you keep your car neat and uncluttered, you're less likely to be the cause of an accident. This will greatly benefit your safety, well-being, and auto insurance costs.

14. MAINTAIN A QUEST-FRIENDLY HOME: You won't have to worry about moving things around before invited guests or uninvited ones appear.

15. HEALTHIER EATING HABITS: You can develop healthy eating habits by implementing a minimalist lifestyle in your kitchen, store, and refrigerator.

If you have a few healthful basics and fresh meals in your kitchen, you won't be tempted by nibbles from your cupboard or freezer.

16. INVESTING YOUR MINIMALIST SAVINGS: There are several methods in which minimalism and cost-cutting go hand in hand, enabling you to gradually save a bigger portion of your income.

Savings can be used to improve one's financial decisions, such as starting a new investment portfolio or raising retirement contributions.

17. FEEL AT EASE IN A SMALLER PLACE: Living in a smaller room with fewer belongings makes you feel more at ease and can save a lot of money.

18. MAKE ROOM FOR YOUR INTERESTS AND HOBBIES: You can spend more time engaging in your favorite hobbies and

interests by reducing the space you use for storage at home.

19. START A NEW CHAPTER IN YOUR LIFE: Living a minimalist lifestyle allows you to turn a new page.

Eliminating clutter, disarray, and disorder can help you start the next chapter of your life.

20. LETTING GO OF YOUR PAST: Getting rid of things that trigger bad memories may be fairly calming, even though it's still a good idea to have a few items in your home that remind you of joyful times.

You can prevent unpleasant emotional triggers by removing the tangible objects that bring you down.

Chapter 3: MINIMALISTS' BRANCHES AND TYPES

Owing to the differences and variations in the model that alter how different people perceive the minimalist idea, it has spread to various classes. People interpret minimalism differently, and as a result, it is understood that they cannot be grouped into a single class. The underlying principle, however, is the less-is-better maxim that characterizes all forms of minimalism.

Among the branches of minimalism that have emerged are the following:

Thrifty Minimalism

They share waste-conscious habits with sustainable minimalists, but the underlying aims of the economical minimalist are entirely different. They can be seen taking care of their gardens, shopping at thrift stores, and redecorating furniture, but the main goal is to cut costs rather than use loans. They adopt minimalist tendencies due to their financial constraints. They are frequently found in small apartments or, at the very least, paired up with roommates to save on rent. However, frugal minimalists are known to hang onto things as much as they can fit to avoid needing them later on and having to pay to buy the same thing again. The frugal minimalist views it as a waste of time, particularly if the object's quality isn't up to par.

Exemplary Minimization

The apex of experiential minimalism is the conviction that the quality of experiences matters infinitely more than the quality of objects. Therefore, the experiential minimalist owns a few items, not because he wants to collect or cure things but because of his lifestyle. You may also refer to them as "backpackers" because of their capacity to pack their entire lives into a bag and be prepared for anything. However, this category of minimalism encompasses a diverse variety of individuals, from thrill-seeking hippies to freelance digital natives.

Suĕtainable Minimalists: The term "green minimalist" refers to the sustainable, minimalist movement. Their focus lies in living a green lifestyle, which reduces consumption, dependence, and environmental harm. If it implies they desire less, they will possess more belongings, including more clothing, land, and toys. They may be found leading a homestead life, or at least wishing to, since their priorities are focused on minimizing waste and using the land to the greatest extent possible. This kind of minimalism is sometimes more considerate of the environment as it's all about preserving the individual and their way of life. The maxim guides the sustainable, minimalist movement: "make do, or do without."

Crucial Minimization

The goal of fundamental minimalism is to determine just how little a person can live without, which is why many are experimenting with living without stuff. They are obsessed with using, creating, and narrowing down their affiliations to the best. Look into their kitchen cabinets or closets to find a scarce collection-scarce collection sufficient to last for a week or so before the next wash. In the minimalist's mind, quantity and quality are more important than waste; occasionally, they will part with their old items to acquire better, more valuable ones. If they only purchase one, it must be the best and last the longest. Therefore, they make every effort to purchase the best item within their means.

Visual Minimalism

All that matters is what their eyes can perceive and enjoy, so long as the minimalist style is considered. They don't exactly own lesions, but they do have lesions on show. Their preferred color for walls, windows, dinnerware, everything, and most of all, is white. Since it's all about the visuals, it's simple to determine the aesthetic minimum. Once you step through the front door of their colorless apartment, all you will see are bare countertops, bare floors, and naked walls—perhaps except one little piece of abstract art carefully placed atop a shaker-style bench.

Conscientious Minimalism

A Mindful minimalist finds joy and spiritual enlightenment in purging unnecessary items. They employ acceptable moderation solely for their peace of mind, not for specific self-serving or beneficial economic, ecological, or aesthetic reasons. For the mindful minimalist, letting go of their possessions usually means letting go of burdens, guilt, or other negative emotions. Eliminating excess allows the mindful person to better appreciate their intelligence, place in the world, and community while finding greater meaning in their day-to-day existence.

Why Reduce?

What does adopting a minimalist lifestyle entail? What is this "minimalist" way of living? To live a minimalist lifestyle, or to embrace minimalism, is to get rid of everything unnecessary or wasteful; that is, to own necessities and toss the rest. A minimalist lifestyle can help you make more room or time for the things that matter to you and make it beautiful, such as experiences, relationships, and other things that provide true worth to your life.

A simple lifestyle may be incredibly energizing and freeing. By doing this, you can replace all of the noise and confusion in your life with tranquility and mental clarity. Additionally, living a minimalist lifestyle will considerably assist you in making the most of the time you have available to accomplish the activities and spend with the people that truly bring you profound joy and happiness.

A minimalist lifestyle can, however, also feel daunting at times, especially when first embracing it. This is due to the likelihood that you will discover many unnecessary items in your life that you need to get rid of. You may not know where to start because you will likely need to let go of many things in your life. Although adopting a minimalist lifestyle is not easy or simple, you can take continuous baby steps toward your goal if you remember that everything worthwhile in life requires time and effort.

A lovely way to visualize shifting to a minimalist lifestyle is to turn a cup upside down and visualize everything falling away, leaving only the important things. And from this angle, it's critical to understand what minimalism isn't. To begin with, minimalism does not mean discarding everything that holds sentimental value. Secondly, the idea here is not to deny or deprive oneself of the experiences and things that might make life more beautiful and fulfilling. A minimalist lifestyle, commonly called minimalism, is a way to focus more of your attention on the most fulfilling and significant aspects of your life. It may involve letting up of things and people who provide you little to no value. By doing this, you'll be able to make more time and space to enjoy the important things, boosting your happiness and sense of fulfillment. Therefore, you'll be pleasantly pleased to learn that minimalism is about liberation or freedom, even if you still think it's a lifestyle of self-denial or repression.

Minimalism also does not entail a moral code or compass. Eliminating some items and relationships from your life does not automatically make them bad or immoral. It all comes down to fulfilling your mission to lead the happiest and most contented life possible. Coincidentally, more isn't necessarily better regarding such a goal. Having too much of anything may be extremely detrimental and unsatisfying. After finally adapting to a minimalist lifestyle, you will have a wonderful sense of freedom from materialism, one of the world's most enslaving beliefs or values.

Entity Minimization

The essential minimality drives them to discover exactly how much they can live without. They are obsessed with having less, consuming less, and reducing their possessions to the essentials. Look inside their kitchen cabinets or closets for a short-supported collection – just enough to last until the next wash. Their minimalistic mindset does not usually prioritize waste over quality and quantity; essentialists occasionally discard their old items in favor of better, more valuable ones. They use all their resources to purchase the best item they can afford; if they only purchase one, it must be the greatest and last a lifetime.

Signature Motion: Bring out a mere twelve necklaces for their carefully chosen seasonal wardrobe.

They could adore substituting audiobooks or electronic periodicals for their regular reading materials.

Proficient Minimalists

The foundation of experiential minimalism is the belief that experiences' quality matters more than objects' quality. Therefore, even though the expert has few personal preferences, it's more of a sign of their chosen lifestyle than the result of deliberate curating. You may also refer to them as "backpack minimalists" because they can pack their entire lives into a backpack and be prepared for everything. However, this particular category of minimalists includes a wide range of personalities, from thrill-seeking hippies to freelance digital nomads.

Signatur Move: Remove their hangers since their entire wardrobe fits within a suitcase.

They could adore trying to acquire a new skill or hobby.

Ecological Minimalism

One might refer to the sustainable minimalist as the eco-minimalist. Their focus lies in green living, which reduces consumption, dependence, and environmental harm. They will own more items, such as tools, land, and clothing, if they want less. They may be found enjoying a homestead life, or at least retiring to one, since their main concerns include minimizing waste and spending as little time on the land as possible. This kind of minimalism sometimes cares more about improving the environment than improving the individual and their chosen lifestyle. "Make do, or do without" is the motto that propels the sustainable, minimalist movement.

Signature Motion: crafting their necklaces out of recovered wire and wood from their land.

They may adore learning the craft of crafting anything from scratch.

The Whole Advantages Of Living A Minimalist Lifestyle

I want you to complete this exercise in this chapter. Consider a home where each room is covered in patterned wallpaper. Suppose all the rooms have patterned carpets, and the colors don't go well together. The hue of the sofa is dark. When you enter the room, the hue of the walls and the black curtains immediately catch your attention. There are numerous ornaments scattered about, and dust gathers on them all. A few dates back to when the children went on field trips. Some are presents from folks who felt they had good taste. For a brief period, close your eyes and visualize this kind of setting. When faced with a room like this, let alone a mansion full of them, you get the impression that the mind can never find a place to relax. Every room is so crowded that it is difficult to unwind. It is so full of stuff that it is difficult to settle down since you are constantly feeling bad about the condition of the house and the possessions inside.

This may be an exaggeration, but I use it to illustrate the idea that "less is more" as I describe what it's like, on the other hand, to enter a neatly organized home that isn't too furnished or cluttered. A hotel room is generally colorless. It usually has relatively few personal touches and is quite friendly. You quickly realize that you are not at home, but if you pay a reasonable fee for a hotel room, it will be simple, clean, and most definitely functional. This is a step below your home. In addition to being tidy and functional, it should be cozy and contain some of your most treasured possessions. One item that can assist you in decluttering is referred to as a focal point. Close the door and leave the room where you are going to clear. Next, walk inside the room and genuinely observe what immediately draws your attention.

It ought to be the main attraction. For a minimalist family, it may be an artwork. Maybe it's even a brightly colored vase or a plant. But I'll wager that when you walk into a room in your house, the abundance of clutter draws your eyes in all directions, making it difficult to find the area's focal point.

When you declutter, you refocus everything and intentionally set up your space to function as you did when you originally moved into the house. You purge unnecessary things and confirm that everything in the space is meant to be there. You will immediately find your focus points and the space enjoyable, but first, you must win over the entire family. You must establish the following guidelines at home if you want to maintain your minimalist lifestyle:

A room is usually left more orderly after people depart it.

After bathing, folks tidy up and put their laundry in the trash.

When using the restroom, individuals use the brush to ensure that it is clean for the person using it after them.

A child must give up one old toy to receive a new one.

Teens must determine what to give up before receiving anything new.

If children understand that doing this will enable them to follow your example and keep their rooms clean, they will unlikely rebel against you despite your fears. Teens who are allowed this flexibility have been shown to maintain their rooms cleaner than those who are not, thus supporting the concept of room and encouraging them to have a unique style.

Children who learn to cook will inherit valuable skills and understand the importance of consuming high-quality food rather than constantly turning to unhealthy, convenient options. They also enjoy participating in garage sales to raise money for new toys, and they will quickly learn the lesson of excess if it is established that each item brought in must be replaced by one or two that are taken out.

Your home will have a better atmosphere, and you won't feel as pressured daily after work. Because you won't have as much housework, you'll have more time to spend with your children and truly enjoy your vacation. I recommend that you take part of this time to take the kids on a field trip or to a country setting so they can enjoy the outdoors and get enough exercise. Living a simple lifestyle will prevent kids from losing themselves in front of a computer screen and increase their interest in the world around them.

The benefits of minimalism are numerous. It facilitates easier living. It gives your house a brand-new, modern feel. It relieves a lot of your tension related to chores and responsibilities. It turns your house into a delightful place where you can invite guests over on a whim without worrying about cleaning up after them. Additionally, you'll notice that your chances of entertaining and hosting people at your freshly decorated house have increased significantly. If you demonstrate the advantages to them, they're likely to change their way of living because a minimalist home is amazing.

Chapter 6: Simplified Clothes and Personal Hygiene

If you want to incorporate minimalism into your appearance but are unsure where to begin, this chapter will walk you through it. Feeling a bit nervous about altering your personal style is acceptable, particularly if you've always thought minimalist clothing is boring.

However, minimalism opposes wastefulness, and many individuals tend to be very wasteful regarding personal hygiene and attire. Too many clothes, shoes, accessories, makeup, and toiletries that only collect dust due to inactivity are frequently seen. Thus, the following excellent advice will help you strike a balance between minimalism and attractiveness:

The Simplified Clothes

A sense of style can exist without an oversized wardrobe. You may even have items in your closet that you haven't worn in months. Remove every item of clothing from your closet and divide it into three piles: "basics," "seasonal," and "goodwill."

The items of clothing in the basics pile are the ones you wear most often. They are typically the most adaptable items in your wardrobe, matching nearly any other ensemble you own.

Summer and winter clothing are considered seasonal items. You can store them in the attic after packing them into vacuum-sealed bags.

The clothing you haven't worn in over three months should go in the goodwill pile. Take a photo of them for the sake of your memories if they hold sentimental significance, and then give them all to Goodwill.

After going through your wardrobe, it's time to tidy your closet and arrange your essentials. To make things appear attractive and make it easier to find a piece you would like to wear on a given day, you can arrange them according to a color scheme.

You may use the same concept for accessories, purses, and shoes.

Going to a clothing and shoe store should only be done when necessary in the future. Even so, go to a vintage or used goods store rather than making a brand-new purchase. In this manner, you contribute to the "reduce and reuse" movement and save money.

Additionally, the secret to becoming a stylish minimalist is to use creativity when combining simple pieces to create a variety of appearances. Invest in a few well-made, adaptable pieces that complement each other to switch up your wardrobe whenever you feel like it. Generally speaking, buying clothing in the same color family will make it easier for you to mix and match them. Earth tones, or browns, reds, yellows, golds, and greens, are warm tones. Jewel tones include shades of pink, purple, blue, and silver. Beige, gray, black, and white are examples of neutral tones.

Simplified Personal Care

Especially for women, grooming can be a laborious ritual involving pots and bottles of creams and potions. Regrettably, this practice can be costly, time- and energy-consuming, and environmentally unfriendly. Most individuals will inevitably need to use toiletries for grooming, so the best course of action is to get rid of the goods you don't use very often if you can't part with them.

Women can, for example, refrain from buying so many makeup items that would, in any case, expire after a few months. Rather than buying a new palette every time she visits the drugstore, she can buy one and use it extensively until it runs out before buying a new one. Moreover, suppose she can locate a product that serves two purposes: a sunscreen foundation or a tinted moisturizer. In that case, it will save her money and time as she won't need to apply many layers of makeup daily.

Men and women can use fewer grooming products by selecting reasonably priced, high-quality, and environmentally friendly body soaps, shampoos, and conditioners. Investing in reusable razors and refillable containers rather than disposable ones can help you lessen your carbon footprint.

Recall that maintaining hygiene and dressing nicely doesn't have to be difficult. Above all, remember that your confidence is the finest accessory.

It Doesn't Have To Cost More To Be Minimalist

Bite-sized trends are the foundation of our culture: two-paragraph Facebook rants gain traction, six-second videos top "trending" charts, and tweets become viral as people start receiving widespread exposure for their content. As a technologically savvy society, we take great satisfaction in our capacity to publish content that can be read in under a minute and get enough attention to be deemed "viral." We find ways to keep going to consistently develop a following of individuals who can stroke our egos because this fleeting outpouring of love and affection is enough to make us feel good about ourselves because other people think we're worthwhile.

Put another way, we've discovered a means to measure our value based on material objects that people use to fully expose their lives.

The concept of "trending" is closely linked to the requirement that something be visually appealing. If the message is not verbally visceral, things in style typically have a visual element. This means that filtered images, collage videos, and even picture and video albums get the greatest attention since they appeal to multiple senses simultaneously and establish an emotional connection between the viewer and the creator.

This implies that if a concept, way of life, or philosophy is "trending," it has a visual component attached to communicate its meaning without requiring the reader to read a long text—especially if it takes more than 30 seconds.

For instance, numerous books detailing the best places to buy fuzzy socks, where to get the cheapest candles, and what designs were the most soothing to use on blankets were released when the hygge lifestyle started to gain popularity in the United States. The hygge lifestyle is unrelated to those items; rather, they are symbols of a particular culture that originated from the Danish way of life, reflected in their morals and climate—

Denmark can be gloomy, bitterly cold, and isolating at times. Therefore, even though they associate the hygge lifestyle with things like candles and warm socks for their feet, the idea of "keeping warm to be comfortable" would not be appropriate to help someone unwind in a setting like Spain in the middle of July.

Therefore, when the minimalist idea started to "trend" in the US, it was accompanied by the same visually stimulating images featuring recurring items that people believed were essential to the lifestyle: boyfriend sweaters, baggy cardigans, long, monotone coats, blocked colors, baggy shirts, and even plain leggings. Individuals started to disregard the concept of "minimalism" and its philosophy in favor of "appearing the part." Individuals lost sight of the need to downplay the unimportant things and emotions in their lives. They were obsessed with a "trending look" to attract more followers and help them develop their "viral brand."

Do not fall into the trap that our society presents with such beliefs. When executed correctly, minimalism incurs no expenses. Your home won't cost you anything to declutter. It costs nothing to reduce the size of your wardrobe. It costs nothing to get rid of some of your extra furnishings.

Why? Since these things are not being replaced. You are permanently discarding them to live a simpler life that places less value on material possessions and more on observing and being present in the world around you.

Some people see a minimalist lifestyle as a total overhaul of their way of life. They start by purging their homes and fall so deeply in love with the concept that they decide to sell their houses, break their leases, and move on the road. Motorhome living is the most common type of on-the-road lifestyle, but for many people, it can mean packing a big van with a few essentials and hitting the road.

No matter what kind of lifestyle you decide to follow on your minimalist journey, it shouldn't come with a high financial penalty.

Decluttering is free for people who just want to organize their belongings. Subsequently, suppose you have essential objects that still require a home. In that case, plenty of thrift stores offer inexpensive furniture and filing cabinets to those who do their decluttering and donation. If you need anything to assist in organizing vital items like birth certificates and paper documents, never undervalue the deals you can discover in a thrift store.

It still doesn't have to cost much money if you want to fully commit to living a minimalist lifestyle and selling everything you possess to work from home and travel the country. Look through all your contacts to get a used car that is in good operating order. Buying secondhand instead of going into a lot and buying something from a sales floor will save you thousands of dollars. Just be sure you are knowledgeable enough to thoroughly inspect the car to avoid being saddled with something that will break down in two months.

If someone tries to persuade you that adopting a minimalist lifestyle costs money upfront, they are completely missing the mark. Giving up material belongings and pointless items is not only a selfless act but can also result in financial savings down the road. Many downgrade to smaller phones and phone plans; many drop cable and several of their streaming services; others even downgrade to smaller homes. These practices follow the principles of a minimalist lifestyle and put money back into your pocket.

Chapter 6: Organizing Your Financial and Professional Life

How To Clear Out The Clutter In Your Finances

Take these steps to clear the clutter in your financial life:

Control Your Spending: Examine each of your fixed and variable costs. Food, medication, health insurance, vehicle maintenance, travel expenses, basic clothing, rent, utility bills, and education (if you are enrolled in school or have children) belong in that group.

Examine your income and expenditures for the various extras in life now. It's an extra and pointless purchase if you can't even pay your basic bills, buy a new device every month, and take out a loan from a friend to make that purchase. Determine various costs of that kind and gradually begin to reduce them.

If you buy new clothes every month for $200, for example, reduce that amount to $150 or $180, then gradually reduce it to $20 or even less. Start building your savings by putting the money in a piggy bank or savings account.

Launch a Prohibition on Shopping:

Make a self-promise to stop buying more than you truly need going forward.

Do not get two phones if you can live with just one, as this will raise your costs.

Don't buy a new toaster just because you like the design if you already have one that works fine.

Make a self-promise to buy just what you need so that you can begin living with fewer possessions. Gradually transform your commitment into a shopping ban, keeping track of all your purchases. Before making a purchase, consider whether it is necessary, and then note your findings in your journal. Review it frequently to assess how well you are keeping your word and identify any areas where you need to improve. You'll soon be increasing your funds and making fewer purchases than before. Ask yourself, "Is there something better I can do with X dollars (the amount of the object you want to buy)?" before making any purchases. This will enable you to view your purchase from a more favorable angle.

Purchase a Reputable Savings Plan: Throw away all your credit cards because they sometimes lead to impulsive purchases. While doing so, select one or two reputable savings plans and allocate a portion of your funds to them. You will benefit from these plans in an emergency.

Making these adjustments will not come easily at first. Still, as you take small steps toward your goals, you will feel better and become more driven, gradually incorporating minimalism into your daily life.

Let's now examine how you might simplify your work life.

How To Incorporate Minimalism Into Your Career

Here are some tips for simplifying your work life.

Examine Your Activities Related to Your Work: Go over your professional responsibilities and activities first to see if there are any extra or pointless ones. For example, if you work two jobs and the income from one of them suffices to cover your personal and household costs, you can eliminate the burdensome second job and free up more professional time.

Reduce Your Extra Activities Gradually: Once you've determined which of your many professional pursuits are depleting your quality of life, begin gradually reducing them. First, reduce your spending if you wish to leave one of your two jobs. You'll quickly discover you don't need two jobs when you start saving more, and you'll be able to leave one of your employment.

Never Accept More Work Than You Can Complete: Additionally, refrain from accepting more projects and assignments than you can manage. You know the workload you can do easily; try not to exceed that amount. Talk to your boss and come to a reasonable conclusion if you have just finished a successful project and they want you to take on another one and finish it by an unrealistic deadline.

Establish Insightful Career Objectives: Examine your career objectives throughout time to determine whether the ones you currently have still have value. Establish one or two worthwhile goals immediately if you haven't set any or have never done so. Consider your capabilities and abilities and what you truly want to accomplish to create a few relevant life goals. Go after such objectives gradually to add value to your work life.

Making these changes may take some time, so be kind to yourself. You'll notice a noticeable change in your life over time. Integrate simplicity into your health to maintain that fantastic sensation.

Acquiring The Viewpoint Of A Minimalist

It is no secret that materialism and consumerism are the lifebloods of our civilization. Living a minimalist lifestyle is considered counter-cultural because it seems like something many people find too "out of the box." Like all new and strange things, it is one of those terrifying and enigmatic things. Many people have lucrative occupations and generate large salaries, yet they frequently live paycheck to paycheck due to their risky spending habits. Whether we like to admit it or not, we are always over cluttering our lives with inanimate objects because they are the "best new invention" or the "trending thing on the market."

Common Arguments Against Minimalism

A glimpse inside the life of a minimalist reveals contented individuals who are content with having fewer material belongings. There are many arguments against people incorporating small portions of the minimalist lifestyle into their own lives, even though people of all ages are drawn to owning less, maintaining order, and being content without the need to acquire.

Many people frequently oppose leading a minimalistic lifestyle for the reasons listed below. You should be aware that not everyone will understand why you are subjecting your family to such a "horrific experience" when you set out on this journey, but remember that you are doing this for YOU and YOUR family, not theirs. You are starting to experience the kind of life that they only dream of.

"I don't want to face criticism from others."

People in our culture form their opinions based primarily on our possessions. That is why aiming for a life with less seems so unrealistic. When minimalists say they don't desire goods, many people don't understand. You can be perceived as an outsider for a while, and people will ask you about your decisions. However, time will pass, and they will no longer think of you. Most likely, they are so consumed with what other people think of them that they won't remember that you lead a distinctive lifestyle.

"I frequently overthink things, and there's nothing I can do to stop it."

No, streamlining your ideas is not simple, but it is also not impossible difficult. One of the many reasons people choose to live a minimalist lifestyle is that many were formerly specialists at overanalyzing things. Regular meditation helps us regularly spring clean our minds, making it easier to solve problems that may otherwise seem insurmountable.

"There is no way that I could be content with less."

Yes, at first, it can seem ridiculous to be happier with less in life. It contradicts much of what we are taught and told throughout our lives. Less is more, though. The more things you own, the more time you need to maintain, replace, organize, and clean them. Less gives you more freedom and reduces your stress levels. Additionally, there are exponential financial gains associated with this! Subtracting from your life instead of adding to it is a way that can fix more issues.

Some people find minimalism simple since living with less is in their nature. That's not the life for me!"

That argument might have some merit, yet minimalism is not solely dependent on your personality. It is a deliberate attempt to focus less. Many minimalists used to lead lives similar to yours, full of possessions and complexity. They, too, had a difficult time making the transition to a minimalist lifestyle. However, I can assure you that every step was most likely worthwhile! People who genuinely understand the richness of loving less and preserving that for what matters decide to live with less.

"I'm committed to too many things."

Many operate under the false assumption that we are constantly busy, even when we can do far more with far less. Minimalism is a terrific method to start the practice of time management if you are always on edge due to a lot of overpowering ideas. It shows you how to divide your time wisely and eliminate anything unnecessary for your success and productivity.

"My _____ would disagree with me, even though I would love to simplify."

I understand how difficult it can be to get your partner to agree with you, particularly when changing aspects of your routine that you are accustomed to. Start by identifying areas of agreement, concentrating on the advantages minimalism can provide you both. Start modest and focus on your personal life first. You must determine the line that both of you feel comfortable staying inside. With time, you will learn how to do it.

"What happens if I discard something that I will eventually need?"

The "what if" questions in life only prevent us from taking advantage of wonderful possibilities. But you are not by yourself. I think this is one of the more prevalent issues we all face, particularly when it comes to eliminating unnecessary items in our lives. We strive to foresee the future and get pleasure from doing so. However, nobody can. And we're usually not very good at it when we do try. Get rid of items that can be quickly replaced, and quit arguing with yourself about them.

Sorting Through Your Clothes

1. Get rid of everything in your closet that doesn't fit you well, even if it's now

in style. Give boot-cut pants away if they don't fit your body type. But if long leather skirts suit you well and aren't trendy right now, keep them.

2. Get rid of whatever you have several of. Get rid of the extra six caps if you have ten, but only utilize four.

3. Get rid of anything you've been holding onto for milestones, weight loss or growth, or important occasions. Donating an item to someone who can use it is preferable if you haven't worn it in a long time because you won't wear it again.

4. When you learn to live with less clothing, follow the 2-bag rule: only pack items that will fit into two carry-on bags and two baggage bags. If you follow this

rule, you can wear the clothes you need and want.

Cleaning Up Your Living Room, Dining Room, and Bedroom

1. Get rid of any broken ornaments, ones you don't particularly enjoy, ones you received for free but don't value, ones you know can be replaced with better items, and ones that don't bring you joy or inspiration.

2. Save anything that makes you want to do better, brings back pleasant memories, advances your objectives, or involves things you truly enjoy.

3. Remove any old furniture you can replace with more durable options. But if an old piece of furniture still has value for you and you're okay with it, keep it.

Organizing Your Device Area and CD/Book Rack

1. Sort through your CDs, books, and electronics to see what you haven't used in a long time. Don't get rid of a piece, though, if you use it occasionally and it holds special meaning in your collection.

2. Throw away any stuff you don't plan to use or a couple in poor condition if you don't hoard.

3. If your children have an overabundance of toys, examine what they have and discard outdated, damaged, or broken ones.

To ensure that you only retain needed items, do the same with your kitchenware, linens, toiletries, paperwork, and files. Most individuals overlook decluttering their pantry and refrigerator when decluttering their homes, workstations, and lives. You should practice minimalism in all aspects of your life, including your eating habits. This aspect is covered in the upcoming chapter.

Chapter 5: Health in Minimalism

Regarding health, I was just as guilty as everyone else of expecting the doctor to fix everything. I wanted drops if I had an earache. I needed a remedy if my eyes were hurting. But ever since switching to a minimalist lifestyle, I've discovered that a lot of my daily illnesses are self-fixable. Regarding lifestyle decisions, there are several fundamental guidelines. Convenience foods, for instance, no longer seem convenient to me. They can't be said to be very convenient if they take years off your life! Using an air fryer was one of the best decisions I've ever made. I also decided to limit my vegetable purchases to fresh produce from the farmer's market after observing how rapidly produce in stores went bad! I adore drinking water and just seldom consume alcohol.

Taking care of my posture is another easy lifestyle decision. It is helpful thanks to yoga and meditation, which are now spontaneously occurring. After addressing my posture, all my aches and problems over the years have been resolved. Our lifestyles are the primary cause of many of our life issues. For instance, how many people do you know who claim to be insomniacs or who lament their inability to fall asleep at night? None of them likely suffer from sleeplessness. They simply decide to lead erratic lives and then wait for their bodies to oblige them to sleep when they want. One buddy even disclosed to me that he suffered from a sleep issue. The truth was that he didn't have a set bedtime since he was leading an aimless life. He would go to bed at four, wondering why he wouldn't wake up before lunchtime the following day. That didn't happen when we stayed with him and enforced our schedule.

The following standards are the most crucial when considering all the necessities that the human body needs at its most basic level. I have to evaluate this for several individuals as well as for my lifestyle, and medical experts support these:

- You require eight hours of sleep every night.
- Eight glasses of water a day is necessary for you.
- You must eat wholesome food that is rich in vitamins and minerals.
- Exercise is necessary; even brisk walking counts.

There are thousands of items in your daily life that you don't need but yet use. To help you understand where you are lacking in your lifestyle, allow me to share a few with you:

• Junk food is not necessary in between meals.

There's no need for quick food.

• It's unnecessary to watch TV nonstop—in fact, doing so would lead to information overload.

• Noise isn't necessary all the time.

Although music is often a positive thing, it wasn't the case in my friend's home. There was constant music playing. It was not a selection of songs based on their unique qualities; rather, it was arbitrary. It sounded like a radio all day. His home was much more serene after he adopted a minimalist lifestyle and began to select the music he listened to. To be heard, one did not need to yell.

I'm not kidding when I suggest that watching TV causes information overload. You are constantly subjected to commercials, and while many charity ones aim to raise your awareness of global issues and hardships, you can easily find that information online when you wish to donate rather than being made to feel guilty about your way of life. Every time we sat down to eat, I used to find hungry children rushing in through the TV screen. The issue is in the timing of advertisements. They target individuals, and you are having your life controlled by that screen. I care for and try to assist people in other nations but only do so when it suits me.

Being minimalistic isn't
Following a definition of minimalism and explaining its tenets, the next step in leading a minimalist life is to confront the path of least resistance. Put another way, consider what minimalism is not when defining it.

The easiest method to discover who we are is to define it without conflict or hostility. Consequently, we shouldn't use our differences to determine who we are. In the same manner that parallels have the drawback of making an effort to visualize, we should not define ourselves via them. Additionally, analogies presume a basic portrayal of the past, usually inapplicable to circumstances that aren't always exactly analogous.

On the other hand, it is crucial to define ideas in terms of what they are not to prevent misunderstandings and encourage and stimulate critical thought.

Minimizing does not mean organizing.

Our organization will improve due to minimalism, and our increased awareness of our possessions will follow from improved organization. If we maintain the same quantity of items, having an organizing system or keeping everything in one location is not minimalism. After determining the quantity and value of each component, organizing is a necessary first step before eliminating what is unnecessary.

Arranging and stacking athletic wear in the same area will help us identify the items we own in that category, confirming that we might have excess shirts or sports tights. If, up until now, we have stored them in various locations or placed T-shirts in the bottom of multiple drawers, we have made the error of mistaking what is not visible for what is not real.

We'll notice how simple arranging is if we apply minimalism to various aspects of our lives. And tidy. Conditioning a wardrobe with 20 items differs from conditioning with 40.

Brands, social standing, and ego

Neither generic goods nor brands are favored or opposed by minimalism. Whether or not it has an etched brand, it is a neutral movement in favor of having less.

Minimalism challenges the necessity. This reductionist line of reasoning has the potential to justify the necessity of wearing a logo. Beyond the significance of our belongings, we undoubtedly conclude that there is no connection between their worth and the contributions that brands make, and we will do away with brands as much as we can. We will no longer define ourselves by the things we own or by their brand.

The goal is to preserve what we need, not to find the priciest or most well-liked goods. The best is frequently not what we most need. Sometimes, a brand will give us what we need, and others won't.

Let's take this occasion to see the proportionate link between our defense or fanaticism of an article and its unnecessary nature. We stress its unnecessary requirement and the purpose for its existence more the more money or effort we invest in it. We shall eventually recognize it as a component of who we are. It will cost us more to sever that root and attachment once it has become ingrained in us. Branded goods will highlight this sense of community or kinship with a group.

Consumption is fueled by this identity, supplied falsely by specific items. Boost the rivalry between brands for identity and status. In addition to increasing vulnerability, defining oneself through symbols outside oneself leads to an endless accumulation of material belongings to feed that brittle identity. Everything suffers from comparison; our new clothing is not as stylish as our friend's, and our salary becomes less appealing when we learn about our partner's wage. Crimes of ego. The fundamental notion that we must prove something to someone, even if that someone is ourselves, is embodied in that contentment with the content. Ironically, the perception that a product and its brand convey about us matters only to the degree that people perceive us as actual users of the thing and are aware of its meaning. Therefore, it suggests that we neglect ourselves to concentrate on ourselves, even though, in reality, everyone is staring at the rest of the world. Set in a meeting, we worry that our shirt is the best rather than looking at the other shirts; strangely, everyone in the audience feels the same way, and no one else is noticed except him.

We are neither entirely logical nor entirely rational, and we do not resemble the homo economicus that economics texts portray. As with any complex system, the behavior of the system's various components is just as important as its degree. Thus, it's not that we are all brand names in one way or another, but rather that we will be more brand-sensitive in certain sectors than in others. Nevertheless, we must recognize the thin line separating self-justification from the relationship between deeds and ideas since we live according to our identities. An absolute incoherence between opposed parts is unstable by nature. In this sense, we will undoubtedly value brands in food and technology if we do the same with our clothing.

Let's also maintain minimalism's neutrality and reiterate: if the best solution to a need has a brand associated with it, we neither violate any maxims nor are we being inconsistent in our acquisition of it.

Restricting Options And Remedies

Among the largest time, wasters are indecisions. Rather than delaying your decisions, make better use of your time. The majority of the time, having too many options to pick from leads to hesitation. Minimalism aids in addressing the problem of options.

Start with the various options available to you at home. You can cap how many items of clothing, pants, shoes, purses, electronics, fragrances, and skin care items you own. When choosing what to wear at different times, you won't be as tempted to focus on the patterns of your curtains and bedding if they are solid colored. Always use white for your bathrobe and towels. Making a beverage selection won't be too difficult if you only have water in your refrigerator.

Restrict your options for services to those that people you know have suggested. If your favorite markets, stores, eateries, or theatres can still meet your needs, there's no need to look elsewhere.

You have to restrict options in addition to selections. For example, you don't need the wall kind if your kitchen already has floor cabinets, especially after decluttering.

You also employ, often without giving them much thought, organizers such as drawer dividers, condiment racks, and hangers. You don't need an organizer for your condiments as long as you store them in an organized way on your counter. To make drawer dividers, simply fold your clothes, stack similar ones, and carefully place the stacks on the drawers. You can merely leave room between the piles in place of dividers.

Among all organizers, hangers are one of the most beneficial. To create a more organized closet, you can get them. But you should only have twenty; the less, the better. Anything more just serves as a reminder to hold onto some clothing that you should otherwise discard. One rod is also sufficient for a wardrobe with twenty or less clothing hanging. Purchasing a new pair is not the answer if your shoe rack is too small to accommodate more shoes. Rather, take out one pair and swap them for the ones you bought.

Minimising and Steering Clear of Digital Mess

Limits can also be imposed when selecting which social media applications to utilize. Simply wishing to stay in touch with loved ones? Facebook, Instagram, or other widely used messaging app should work fine. If you're looking for pictures, Pinterest is a good option. YouTube is still the greatest source for educational videos.

On the other hand, a lot of pointless stuff may be found online. But first, you should establish boundaries around the quantity of devices you own and how you use them before discussing how to prevent them. For example, you can continue to use your TV for learning and leisure.

Your home office's desktop PC should only be used for work. Meanwhile, you can use your laptop for personal and professional purposes. (A tablet can be used in its place.) It would seem that owning two phones is in opposition to minimalism. For tax considerations, purchasing a separate phone for work is essential.

A pair of wireless earphones should be sufficient for accessories for your two phones. You can use the standard speakers with your TV and desktop computer. Bluetooth speakers should be ignored. Every other gadget has an integrated speaker, except your TV and desktop PC. With that, you don't need an earbud or a portable speaker to play and listen to music.

Once you've sorted through the various gadgets, be careful to set a time limit for how much time you spend staring at your screen. Stop reading an e-book or watching a movie every thirty minutes to take a break. If you're working, keep it to 30 minutes as well. Next, take a few steps to stand and stretch. In addition, you can get a drink before returning to your work. Try to keep your leisure browsing to no more than ten minutes each day.

Regarding the seemingly limitless options available on the internet, you can consult evaluations and suggestions for films, television series, novels, and music. But confine your search to a single article or website. Another factor to consider is how you're feeling at the time. Why not watch a comedy movie if you're in a good mood? You may choose to listen to relaxing music on wet days. Since the choosing procedure is only a way to pass the time when you have some spare time, don't spend too much time on it.

Keep your social media usage to no more than one or two apps. Set your accounts private if you want to restrict who can see your social media content. Additionally, avoid giving out too many personal details. You most likely have more than 100 connections overall at this stage across all platforms. In case you haven't noticed, the most popular social media networks still encourage you to grow your network.

To get updates from the individuals who are important to you, though, it's still worthwhile to stay. You might unfriend and block a user if you come across multiple offensive posts from them. Remember that you don't have to interact with those who are just friends or acquaintances. Ignore influencers on social media. Cut virtual ties when someone in your network begins to take on that kind of work.

You are welcome to ban individuals based only on their political posts. Reacting to the reaction of others is not worth it. If you're worried about political news, read reputable news websites. Recognize the differences between opinion and news items when you read them. You may live without reading anything about these subjects unless you are employed in the entertainment or fashion industries.

It's possible that advertisers already know a lot about you based on your browsing behavior. Refrain from responding to their online promotional posts to keep them from finding out more. Their advertisements could appear as games, films, images, hashtags, text postings, or even images and photos.

Consider carefully what you post online as well. You can find plenty of sad stories on the internet. Speak with the individual in question or confide in a close friend instead of putting anything confusing online. Refrain from exposing your unclean laundry in words, images, or films.

Ask yourself if it's a decent update about your life and if you can take queries about it before deciding whether or not to submit a photo. Additionally, do this before uploading a video. Ensure the stuff you share from someone else moved or educated you before sharing it. You can choose to report or conceal upsetting stuff you've seen.

Additionally, you should quit participating in pointless groups on social media sites. Only adhere to a group with thoughtful members and frequent updates. That being said, such are uncommon. It's also not worth worrying about looking for one.

You need to take care of alerts next. Turn off the majority of them. Simply glance through the notifications and delete them all each time you launch your social network app. At least once a month, log off of all of your device's browsing activity. Examine your old images from time to time and remove those that you're not comfortable publishing.

Next, take care of your emails. Clear up the spam and trash folders. Examine the many newsletters and social media updates before erasing the remaining emails. Look for the "unsubscribe" option at the bottom of each email after you open one from each sender. The extra alerts from social media are essentially meaningless. In any case, the newsletters are mostly advertising materials.

After reading them and responding to the sender, delete every private email sent to you. Only those relevant to an ongoing project should be kept for work-related ones. Remove the ones that are finished already. Retrieval services are available in the extremely unlikely event that you are asked to provide proof of deleted emails. Although these services are pricey, remember that the likelihood of you needing them is very low.

Computers and phones are useful for more than simply communication; they also increase productivity. You don't need to download so-called productivity apps because they already have built-in clocks, timers, and calendars. Apps that are touted as essential for minimalists aren't required.

It is advisable to keep your personal and work-related files separate. Make a folder for every project to help you organize the files connected to your job. The linked files should then be placed in the same folder. You can organize your files according to various categories (documents, videos, music, and images). Make a folder for each month or year if you have more pictures than you need. For example, your college or high school pictures can be put in one folder. You can also keep ancient family pictures and folders dedicated to your early years.

Keep an eye out for duplicates while organizing your files and removing them. Don't forget to limit your movie and music files. Take ten minutes once every few months to comb through your personal file collection and remove any files you no longer feel significant.

Pay attention to passive revenue to increase your flexibility.

You might want to consider passive income if you truly want to own your time and escape the financial burden of needing a job or the feast-or-famine reality of freelancing. When establishing an asset, you generate passive revenue even if you work on it infrequently or only once. This could be a mailing list, a blog, or an internet store. You just work on it once, in whatever shape it takes, and then periodically maintain it.

You don't need to keep an eye on it constantly. It doesn't require constant supervision to operate. It operates on autopilot. You earn money even while you're asleep when readers purchase a book, sign up for subscription content, click on advertisements, or do anything else you finish monetizing or earning money from.

You automatically generate income. That may sound like a polished pitch from an internet "course" that promises easy money, but it's the truth. To build the system correctly the first time, you must select the appropriate model and put in the necessary labor. If everything goes according to plan, you just have to work on it once, and the money will keep coming in while you sleep, travel, or spend time with your children.

Don't assume that there are only a few specific types of passive income. It doesn't. It could be a blog, an online store, a YouTube channel, software provided as a service, or SaaS. Your creativity is the only thing stopping you from creating new passive revenue streams.

Since online systems typically require less startup money and are easier to automate than offline passive income systems, I would advise you to establish an online passive income system. Purchasing domain names is my preferred passive income strategy.

Real estate and domain names are similar. They increase in value over time; all you need to do is decide which domain names to purchase or remove, and you can sell individual parts of your collection for a respectable annual sum.

Working fewer than seven days a year is not unusual for domain resellers to turn a profit each year. That may sound absurd, but it's the truth. Everything is dependent on your method and level of expertise.

I don't want to scare you, but you must take the time to reach that level. There is a learning curve, as with any company, but certainly, some people sell and acquire domain names while lounging on the beach. You may calculate the hours they work with two hands to determine how many hours they put in to make an annual paycheck. Unbelievable as it may seem, this occurs frequently.

Whatever method you choose, keep your attention on passive revenue. This is the best way to escape the rat race. It's not simple. There will be a few dead ends. You will undoubtedly have to pay for your learning curve, but if you put in enough effort, you will eventually find a solution that suits your unique situation.

The clutter wouldn't disappear with this. Those items will reappear and generate the same quantity of clutter. Furthermore, your mindset would not change.

Developing a mindset that helps you recognize the worth or significance of various aspects of your life is crucial. You can sort items according to priority and eliminate everything that isn't on this list. We refer to this easy procedure as minimalism. There is no way to measure minimalism. The kind of person you are will determine how much downsizing you choose to undertake.

You are on the wrong side of the fence, though, if your goal in adopting minimalism is to better organize your house.

A minimalist home isn't just aesthetically pleasing. It is the total reconstruction of the entire mentality.

Finding and eliminating items from one's life that are unnecessary is the main goal of minimalism. It would result in an entirely clutter-free environment, supporting your increased calmness and productivity.

You need to take a systematic approach to embrace the minimalist way.

Recognize Your Motives

In this world, everything occurs for a purpose. Things often stay in their current state until they are affected by an external influence. The majority of objects in life are subject to this fundamental physics principle. If you think of a minimalist approach, you must have a cause. Your resolve will only become weaker if the reasons are unclear or nonexistent. For the method to succeed in this situation, explaining the "why" is crucial.

Write down your justifications for taking a minimalist approach in a list. It could be anything that motivated you. Perhaps you're tired of your home being so messy. It can be that you can't seem to locate anything inspiring around the house. Perhaps you're spending a lot of time making decisions and want to keep things simple.

There could be a lot of reasons, and each would bolster your determination. But, if you don't have them clear, you'll eventually get complacent, and the chaos will return. You need to explain why you want to live a simpler life. You will always be motivated by these.

Identifying the proper justification for downsizing your house will help you view things differently. Most items that don't fit the bill will appear cluttered if you have a clear reason for owning them, or else they will continue to be belongings that you will struggle to part with.

Continue To Clear Your Clutter

Keeping up consistency with the clutter-elimination process is, of course, the next step after clearing the clutter. If not, you'll have to start over from scratch when the clutter returns. As a result, clearing clutter and taking precautions to ensure it doesn't reappear are ongoing tasks. Let's examine some advice to get you through this:

Look around the house daily: Verify there is no clutter or mess. Before bed each night, ensure the house is tidy and appealing.

Reduce the amount of décor in your living space and bedrooms to keep them clutter-free: The rooms will appear cleaner and larger when you reduce the amount of décor. This is because there are fewer visual distractions nearby. There will be less décor to dust and clean, another benefit of having fewer décor.

Quit shopping: Among all the advice given here, this one could be the most difficult for you. To prevent yourself from buying new things to replace the ones you have thrown out, you must exercise a great deal of self-control and learning. You also need to shop wisely.

So, instead of doing what almost every American does, which is to shop twice or thrice, buy high-quality products that will last. Instead of choosing a set on sale, purchase a set of sofa cushions you truly enjoy. If you adore your décor, there's a good chance you'll stick with it through time.

When shopping, always write a list of the items you need to buy and learn to keep to it. This will ensure that you never forget anything. Making purchases you don't need is certain when you don't have a list when shopping.

Get rid of whatever you don't need for every new item you purchase: Make sure you get rid of everything you do not need before you feel the desire to buy something new, be it a dress, an appliance, shoes, or anything else. This will guarantee that clutter doesn't gradually seep in.

Select quality above quantity: The proverb "quality over quantity" has been repeated so frequently that few people consider it these days. In actuality, though, it will benefit you much in every area of your life. For example, spend on clothing items with exquisite materials and good workmanship rather than storing many items you would eventually have to throw away. You'll have these for a very long time.

Chapter 3: Encouraging Your Partner to Join You

Our children are not the hardest part. People start to follow the new regulations when they realize you mean to enforce them. It is a little easier for them because, for the most part, they don't have access to their own money.

On the other hand, our wives can find it difficult to part with their priceless items. People might believe we are insane. How do you get them to reconsider? You don't.

Sincerity

Take a seat and converse with them. Communicate your feelings to them. Explain to them your motivation for decluttering. This could make it easier for them to appreciate and comprehend your rationale and judgment. They could have overwhelming feelings as they witness the changes accompanying that choice.

It can appear that you are getting rid of significant items. Be truthful when they ask what you are getting rid of and why. Avoid attempting to take items hidden from the house. Avoid attempting to take anything away that is not yours.

Deciding to stop adding new items is the most significant change you can make. Long before people notice that the house appears larger, they will notice that you aren't spending as much money.

They'll notice the cushion in the bank account before they realize that you're letting them hang their clothing in your closet.

Set a good example.

Don't bother them, even if they shop from dawn to dusk. Avoid applying pressure. Try reaching a consensus by allocating a spending cap, for example. Create a different account if necessary.

Try your hardest to clear up any existing clutter in the house, regardless of what is brought in. Your family is more likely to participate once they witness the room starting to change.

You will attract followers if you are a leader. If you cultivate peace, it will come.

Starting in a single place is the optimum course of action. It will demonstrate your progress and allow everyone to observe your accomplishments. That advancement turns into a drug. It is revitalizing and liberating. Both you and everyone else watching get inspiration from it.

If you are the spouse who is protesting

Some spouses give their significant other this book and say, "Here, I want to do this," instead of explaining. What will hurt is the only sensible piece of advice. You'll discover you have more room, perhaps more money, and unquestionably a happier partner.

Give it a go for yourself. Select a wardrobe. Select a box. Clear it out. Remove anything from it that you haven't seen in a long time.

Everything you've outgrown should be discarded. You'll be astounded by how liberating it feels. Your positive attitude is contagious. It has the power to change lives.

Take action if you believe you need to improve your life or are trapped in the same pattern. Make changes to the area surrounding you first.

3. Pay attention to your hobbies and health

You'll have more time to accomplish the things you love—things you never seem to have time for—when you spend less time at Home Depot attempting in vain to keep up with the Joneses.

Although it seems like everyone is complaining about not having enough time, how many individuals take the time to consider how they are spending their days? You might be spending time with your children, going to the gym, doing yoga, curling up with a nice book, or taking a trip. You might be doing whatever you love, but you're stuck at Sears buying more stuff.

4. A reduced emphasis on material belongings

We are only filling a gap with whatever we surround ourselves with; it's all just a diversion. Although it cannot buy happiness, money can purchase comfort. Our fixation with money should end once the initial sense of comfort is achieved.

The media constantly bombards us with promises of happiness via financial pursuits. Our daily struggles are understandable. Defy those desires. That route is hollow and will not bring you happiness.

It's challenging to avoid falling victim to the materialism trap. I have to be reminded all the time that this bliss is illusory. I understand that I don't need things, even though I enjoy them.

5. Greater mental tranquility

Stress results from holding on to material belongings because we constantly worry about losing them. You can let go of your attachment to these things and, in the end, develop a calm, peaceful mind by simplifying your life.

It's that simple: the fewer things you worry about, the more serenity you have.

6. Greater contentment

Happiness follows naturally when you declutter your life because you'll gravitate towards the things that matter. The false promises are easily seen amid the clutter; they act as a breached barrier to the real purpose of life.

Additionally, you will find contentment in increasing your efficiency, focus by realigning your priorities, and delight in taking things leisurely.

i. The Drawbacks of Minimalism

Like anything in this world, there are advantages and disadvantages to everything. We've already talked about the advantages of minimalism; now, let's talk about its drawbacks.

1. Counting All the Time

After adopting a minimalist lifestyle, some people may find that they are constantly counting the amount of each item they own. Some might believe that to maintain this minimalist lifestyle, you must have a limited quantity of each item. As a result, as more goods accumulate, you'll constantly need to reduce your belongings until you run out of room.

To be honest, minimalism isn't just about regularly measuring your possessions and determining if you own less of them. It's about recognizing the value of certain things compared to others that are useless in your life and getting rid of them.

2. Odd Decision

People typically initially perceive you as strange. I like to state that opinions matter not to me, but for those who do, it could take some time to explain to friends, family, and peers why you want to live this lifestyle, and sometimes it takes guts to go against the grain.

3-The Challenging Process of Throwing Things Out

Tossing things away is very simple for some people, while it could be more difficult for others. Rowing away belongings may become a personal and emotional experience for those going through a difficult period.

4-Complacency

Yes, owning fewer things is a requirement of minimalism. But this kind of thinking could lead to complacency. The fundamental tenet of the Own Less movement is that individuals should do less and simply value and be content with what they have. In a way, minimalism could encourage you to set lower goals for yourself.

5-Declutter Addict

Indeed, some people can truly be the complete opposite of hoarders. Rather than preserving whatever you find. Some people even discard nearly everything without considering whether to save the essentials. This is how you can tell if you've turned into an uncluttered person.

6-Unwilling to hang around your location

Even though your friends are wonderful and enjoy your company, they might not want to spend time with you in your home if they discover that you have thrown out practically everything that makes it fun. Usually, they would recommend going somewhere else because all you can do there is sit around.

7. "Just In Case" Please pardon

People may ask you questions such as, "Why did you throw that away?" or "Don't you need those for emergencies?" after giving away most of your belongings. These folks may not get the minimalist movement or your reasons for going in this direction, but it doesn't stop them from always asking you questions and urging you to hold onto supplies in case of crises.

Reduced-Total Productivity

Being Productive, Not Productive. Apply Pareto's Law to bring everything to a boil.

You are busy if your days and nights fly by and you have a large calendar affixed to your refrigerator, crammed with several chores and to-do lists for the next week and weekend. I understand that experiencing a particular moment in life makes you feel alive. However, it is true that constantly being busy gives us the impression that we are on the right track. But at the end of the day or over the weekend, it simply hits us that I haven't finished everything, particularly the most important things. Doing less and accomplishing more is the main goal of a minimalist lifestyle. Thus, allow me to present the idea of being Effective rather than Efficient. These two are very different from one another. Doing the right thing is the key to effectiveness.

Additionally, efficiency is carrying out tasks correctly. Therefore, being productive does not necessarily mean doing everything and doing it well. What do you think? Nothing matters in the end. Then, there is the well-established idea of Pareto's Law of 80/20. All you need to do is apply Pareto's Law to every task you have for the day. Make sure to eliminate and narrow down to 20% of the most crucial jobs that will yield 80% of the intended results. By making the appropriate decisions, you can increase your productivity with the help of this law.

Time management is obsolete; there's no use scheduling time for everything on your to-do list; you'll simply run out of time and most likely burn out completely. Utilise Pareto's Law, sort, and reduce to the top 20% of jobs to complete daily. You will be more productive than ever if you follow through on it. Therefore, cease overloading oneself with work by adding assignment after task to your calendar. If you keep pushing yourself to the limit and creating stress hormones by attempting to achieve everything, you'll probably have a nervous breakdown.

Thus, always remember to be Effective rather than Efficient.

After reading this information, don't let your calendar determine your life's purpose. You will have more time to pursue your interests outside of work. Do what brings you happiness and pursue your hobbies. Doing something you detest is never justified. Be efficient and dedicate time to the things you want to do. Your value should stem from keeping yourself occupied and completing all the chores related to the needless things you burden yourself with to the point of self-defeating. Just focus on the most important things and lead a life apart from the world of busyness. With this understanding, you'll learn to appreciate the finer things in life and feel a lot happier with yourself. Thus, put in a lot of effort, alter your perspective away from the exhaustion of being busy, and always strive to be effective.

It could be tempting to digitally catalog your stuff to deceive. I just preserve their photos to cling to the memories, not the actual objects. You might tell yourself an excuse like that but don't accept it. Remain resilient. There should be no hoarding at all, which also extends to digital items. It's not only about how much room your condition's resultant items take up in your house; it's also about getting rid of the want to keep things longer than necessary.

You may be able to donate a good portion of what you own. As previously noted, items just lying around your house, such as electronics, clothes, shoes, jewelry, and other items, might be used by someone else. Give these things to a thrift store in your area so they might be used. Once more, fill up your automobile and drive to your neighborhood recycling and waste management facilities to eliminate any unnecessary temptation related to the other items you are trash and haven't previously disposed of.

Once most of your belongings have been disposed of, look around to see if anything else can be donated. Have friends and family willing to assist you in conducting a once-over of your house to determine what items you still have that can be thrown away. Refuse to give everything you get rid of to your friends and family. You want to eliminate these things from your life, which is why you do this. Additionally, providing them to those in your vicinity may result in your coming across them and rekindling your hoarding impulse. For instance, you wouldn't want to visit a friend's house one day and discover that one of your twenty-odd lamps is now resting on their end table.

You've now overcome the obstacle. Even if your journey is not quite finished, you have completed the most challenging tasks in releasing yourself from the grip that this unpleasant condition has over you by following the instructions in this chapter. The following chapter will look at how to get rid of materials you have acquired over the years that are particularly strange or harmful.

Individual Connections

Upon examining the practical applications of this lifestyle in interpersonal interactions, it becomes evident that a closer connection with those you love is unavoidable. Your connections with others will improve because you release yourself from pointless and useless belongings. The clarity of your relationships then becomes apparent, and you may even start cutting those who don't support you out of your life. It's unhealthy to spend time with negative individuals, and you might be more negatively impacted than you realize by their negative attitudes and actions, which are harmful to your inner self. This is why having a clear, uncluttered mind is crucial since it makes it easy to spot things, like toxic relationships, that shouldn't be in your life. Finally, setting aside more time and prioritizing fostering stronger family ties is good for mental and emotional health.

Efficiency and Structure

After you have finished decluttering, you will have more time for productivity. You can reorganize your schedule and improve to-do lists when you have extra time to work with. This increases productivity and allows you to accomplish more. The key takeaway is that having more time translates into being more dynamic and driven to pursue your passions rather than just finding the time to do them. A minimalist lifestyle would undoubtedly free up time for important things like hobbies, health, family, or introspection for your well-being.

Now that the idea and advantages of minimalism have been clarified, let's talk about how you may shift to being one. So, how ought one to approach this? In the next chapters, we'll discuss what you can do to start reaping minimalism's rewards.

To put it simply, disarray is synonymous with loose ends. It seems like everything is around you—items that you don't need or love, disorganized items, an excess of stuff, a small amount of space, and a tonne of unresolved business matters—unanswered emails, a DVD that you should have returned long ago, gifts you didn't need, unopened mail and paperwork, broken lightbulbs, a decision or project you keep putting off, items you're not sure you need, old pictures and postcards stashed in a box under your bed. This friend is waiting for your advice about a get-together, dirty toys in the basement, etc. There is an infinite list.

Stress, sadness, and resentment arise when one fails to see the big picture of unresolved issues (disorder). Loose ends are unsightly, drain our vitality, and make us feel heavy and uninspired. It will not be won over, no matter how hard we try to trick our subconscious. On the other hand, we will feel liberated and in control if we simply have a few loose ends to tie up and put them down on an overseeable to-do list to prevent us from losing control. How can we easily accomplish this goal? Using simplicity. We completely tidy and reduce everything, allowing everything to pass through the minimalism filter. The few items that still serve us now are necessities or are dear to us remain.

It's enjoyable to tidy in the merciless minimalist style! Why? Because it's a one-time process that leads to a life of freedom and carefreeness. After cleaning everything once, you will let go of the extras, quickly designate "parking places" for the remaining things, and return utilized goods to their proper locations (more on later).

You will also be astonished at what you find and learn—things you had hardly glanced at before but that may suddenly prove valuable. Enjoy your journey of discovery that is cleaning up! In the past, clients of mine have discovered objects during the cleanup process that they had assumed they had misplaced, or they have discovered a priceless relic whose sale price paid for the minimalism coaching.

It's false to believe that someone is inherently dirty, that they don't have time to clean, or that they can't be creative in a space that has been cleaned up. One can learn how to clean up properly. The proper minimalistic cleaning method entails doing a one-time outside and interior cleaning, freeing up more time for necessities. With the aid of the minimalism filter, minimalism is for people who want to achieve the most with the least amount of work: order, maintaining constant neatness and organization, and feeling free and easygoing.

There is a proverb that goes, "A person who maintains order is simply too lazy to look!" Do you find this to be the case? Would you like to keep squandering your time looking for things? Would you rather continue to feel ashamed whenever uninvited guests drop by your home? What would it be like to surround yourself with things you enjoy and use daily while living in a minimalist setting? Everything is easily accessible, under control, and in its proper position. You adore having unexpected guests because it liberates and gives you energy. Because you've arranged your ideas, you also feel like your head is clear. All of the above are achievable with minimalism, but only if you put in the necessary effort. You will be guided there by the upcoming chapters.

According to psychologists, it might take a person up to thirty days to learn a new behavior or modify an old one. Because humans are adaptable, you can get used to having everything in its proper place and returning items to their original locations after using them. The minimalism filter, which keeps just the things in your life that are genuinely important (my aim), will take some getting used to. So allow yourself some time to become used to the methods outlined here!

It benefits the environment more.

Your actions can have unfavorable effects in addition to the positive ones you can have on this earth and its inhabitants by being compassionate. You commit to reducing your carbon footprint and being trash-aware when choosing a minimalist lifestyle. Sell your toast to someone and spare them the effort of traveling to the store to buy a new one for twice as much. You can always donate your belongings if you don't want to sell, taking one person who supports consumerism off the rolls. Recall the three Rs: Reduce, Reuse, and Recycle if you cannot sell or donate your stuff. These are the values that minimalism and, ironically, environmentalism uphold. If you stay put, I'll give you some pointers on minimizing, reusing, and recycling so that you can have less environmental impact.

A Well-Grounded Method

It takes maintenance to become minimalist, much like with a healthier diet. I started reading and learning about healthy eating because I could not, and would not, see a dietician for the rest of my life. I still require nudges and wise counsel to avoid putting on the weight again. I am less likely to put the weight back on entirely because of my experience in that area, but I still need to exercise caution. I'm unable to eat anything I want to without gaining weight. Sweets are still my favorite, but I must be cautious because of my medicine. The upside is that we can correct course quickly if we veer off course. The same holds for any habit or practice, and minimalism is only one.

Including Minimalism in a Healthful Way of Living

A minimalist lifestyle offers several advantages. One of the easiest and most effective ways to do a project is to go minimalist. It is a fantastic method to lower stress and enhance your fitness and health. It's because many people have a bad perception of well-being and health. They spend a lot of time and money on dangerous weight control programs, joining fitness centers, risky enhancements, and other illicit activities because of the influence of the media and advertisements. They think that without undergoing these difficult operations, they cannot be well. This is untrue. Eating less can help us feel better about ourselves and be healthier.

As the new year begins, we're inundated with messages, ideas, and considerations regarding simple, quick fixes and methods. Avoid them altogether and concentrate on the minimalist approach to greater health if you want to be healthy. The following advice will help you apply minimalism:

1. As much as you can, move it.

Going to an exercise center or completing a required routine to perform bodyweight exercises is unnecessary. Before or after work, these can be completed at home. You can benefit from having the flexibility to work from home. Your cycle of work is ready for you. Utilize it to achieve your objectives. Dependability in employment is crucial. Every day, you should spend 20 to 30 minutes moving your body. There are numerous conceivable results. You can look for stops in the area or just explore without concern for where you could end up.

2. Consume actual food

Food needs to be as crispy as it gets. A simple diet of nutritious fruits, veggies, and nuts will help you reenergize your body. You can consume this nutritious cuisine while working. Dairy products are thought by many to be the finest for supplements. That being said, this is untrue. Your body may become hypersensitive and develop sinusitis if it doesn't recognize dairy products. If you feel at ease with them, it's preferable to consume them. Many packaged foods and comfort foods have additives to make them last longer. You can steer clear of these foods by eating a low-key diet. Don't feel like you have to give up everything that tastes good. Indulging in your favorite unhealthy dish on special occasions like birthdays and holidays is acceptable. It should be carried out periodically.

3. Take a nap

After a demanding workday, you must offer your body rest to attain tranquility. In a society concerned with finishing tasks as soon as possible, taking a break has become seen as indifferent. You are free to skip exercise on Sundays. The second crucial action item is to abstain from using a computer or phone on Sundays. You are able to let go of everything electronic, discover inner tranquility, and experience happiness.

4. The freedom from deceit comes from minimalism.

Even though they don't mean to, many individuals fall for trickery. Their social circle comprises neighbors, coworkers, families, and friends. It is required of them to relate to an outside image that is subservient to their situation. It forces individuals to put in more effort and increases the likelihood that they may lead parallel lives. If you live an honest life, you can lead a stable and constant life. This way of life can accommodate any circumstance. It is simply done on Friday night. It's the same on Sunday morning as it is on Friday. It is dependable, trustworthy, comfortable, and simple to use. In any circumstance, it is dependable, accountable, and informed.

Step 2: Clear the clutter

Decluttering is a step towards minimalism, not a goal unto itself, as previously mentioned. Having said that, if you've been leading a typical modern life, you will surely need to declutter not just your living areas but also your thinking, your social network, your obligations, your hobbies, and every other aspect of your existence.

Thankfully, minimalism is not restrictive; it gives you the freedom to decide what matters to you and what you should and shouldn't keep in your life. This has consequences since minimalism avoids telling you what to keep, throw away, sell, or donate, even if decluttering is a crucial part of living a minimal existence.

Since decluttering is the most painful stage on the minimal route, take your time and deliberate while deciding what to keep and discard. Ideally, you should ask yourself whether something is sentimental or valuable or if you need or use it as you move from room to room, activity to activity, and item to item. You would be better off without something if it does not enhance your quality of life or if you are not using it.

Consider everything in your life because you believe you might need it after clearing out everything you don't need from every area of your life (including your tasks and friendships).

We frequently hoard items we might need at some point in the future; the only problem is that these items typically collect dust in the attic, garage, and corner. If such items are in your life, give them significant thought and get rid of whatever you haven't used in a month, as well as yourself. Ideally, you should hide everything else for a month and keep the items you need. Take out only what you need, and after three months, donate, toss, or sell anything you haven't used. Create your perfect, simple existence with the inspiration and drive this prospect gives you.

The best method to lead a minimal life is to continually remind yourself that getting rid of everything you don't need will make your life simpler, richer, and full of worth, freedom, and fulfillment. Never forget that you get to define minimalism how you see fit because it's a personal decision. Great if all you need is a laptop and a bed. Great if it's an expensive but tastefully furnished home; minimalism is a personal choice, so embrace it.

Conserves Cash

It seems obvious to choose this when it comes to minimalism. You'll have more spare money on hand the less you buy and do. Apart from that, minimalism encourages deliberate action, so you won't have to worry about impulsive purchases. Furthermore, when you locate it, you will have the funds to purchase whatever you genuinely desire.

Increased Self-Belief

"Feeling good about yourself because you have the trendiest clothes, are famous or popular" is one distorted definition of self-confidence. You will have achieved a higher degree of self-confidence if you can feel confident in yourself without requiring any of these things.

Just think of how liberating it would be to maintain your sense of self-worth without all those attachments. You can value who you are more than what you own when you live a minimalist lifestyle.

Having a minimalist mindset

Living simply is a way of life. This implies that to be a minimalist, you must adhere to minimalism in all facets of your life. Everything relates to who you are and how you live, including your place of residence, possessions, social interactions, daily activities, purchases, profession, and aspirations. But keep in mind that you define your own life.

The great thing about minimalism is that you can start anywhere, no matter how much you want to alter your life! Go ahead and focus on your profession or relationships if you believe that's what's best. It's acceptable as long as it gets you there. The fact is, though, that starting is much simpler when you know where to start.

I'm going to presume that since you're interested in minimalism, you have a clear motivation for wanting to adopt a simple lifestyle. This ought to be your initial course of action if you don't. Once you have a clear understanding of your motivation for wanting to live a minimalist lifestyle, you may implement minimalism in your life by doing the following actions, which are covered in more detail later in the book:

Step 1: Decluttering – Eliminating Extra Items

Your first step should be to take care of your own affairs or the things that are entirely under your control because they are the easiest to achieve.

Step 2: Ending unhealthy connections

You can now address your relationships with other individuals after getting your affairs in order.

Step 3: Pursuing a job as a minimalist

Taking care of your affairs and others will help you clear your head and concentrate on choosing a career. It is recommended to reserve the best for last because this phase demands serious concentration.

Chapter 9: The Relationship Between Sustainability and Minimalism

Adopting a minimalist lifestyle has numerous advantages. It can benefit the environment in addition to helping to clean out mental and physical clutter. We will examine the relationship between sustainability and minimalism in Chapter 9 and how leading a more purposeful life might lessen human effect on the environment.

Given that our planet's resources are limited and that we are already beyond many of its boundaries, it is obvious that our existing way of life is not sustainable. Consumption, or the idea that success and happiness depend on a never-ending supply of things and services, is one of the main causes of environmental deterioration.

By encouraging a more deliberate and straightforward way of living, minimalism provides an alternative to consumerism. We may cut back on consumption and waste by eliminating stuff that doesn't add value or happiness to our lives and concentrating on those things. Purchasing durable, high-quality goods rather than inexpensive, throwaway ones, for instance, conserves resources and lessens the need for frequent replacements. We can also decrease our environmental effects by consuming seasonal, locally sourced food and limiting our use of excessive packaging.

Buying used goods rather than brand-new ones, walking or bicycling instead of driving, and using less water and electricity are just a few of the eco-friendly habits that minimalism may promote. Our energy use and carbon emissions can be reduced by downsizing to smaller dwellings and occupying less space.

Awareness of our trash and looking for methods to reduce, reuse, and recycle are essential to living a sustainable lifestyle. This is in line with minimalism, which advocates a minimalist way of living in which things are used until they are no longer functional and possessions are carefully chosen. For instance, rather than just dumping away outdated equipment, think about selling it and giving it to a good cause. Instead of ending up in the trash, clothing can be recycled into cleaning clothes or given to needy people. We may improve our environmental impact by being more conscious of our waste and consumption.

The idea is to eliminate an asset whenever you acquire one that is more important or necessary to you. You may opt to assign yourself a sequential number or choose to completely ignore this tactic. If you decide to use this method, you must inventory everything you own and assign a number. When you reach your breaking point, you have to make the difficult decision of what will survive.

Cutting Down on Your Schedule and Obligations

Minimalism may be applied to real objects, but remember that there are many more applications for it. If you believe you are always rushing, never have enough vacation time, or maybe overly committed, think about scheduling your time and committing to things in moderation.

Of course, whether they are related to it or not, a few items will be standard practice. We could list many activities we could live without, such as work, errands, cleaning, or grocery shopping. Seeing how we allow some things to rule over aspects of our lives that shouldn't be in control is amusing. For instance, you can feel obligated to attend a gathering even though you would prefer not to because you were persuaded to do so. On the other hand, it's also possible that you chose to take charge of a project or club even though you didn't want to, submitting because you knew what was expected of you. Reclaim your hours by adhering to one simple guideline and keeping your schedule within certain bounds. Learn how to decline requests with grace. Express your feelings honestly and tell them that it's not really for you—at least not now.

While some people may take your response in stride and go on, others may take great offense. It's okay; you will never be able to fully satisfy everyone. Your new venture with limitations suggests that you should identify what is typically important to you and eliminate as much of the unnecessary as is reasonable. Even though someone else might not understand your perspective, why would it be wise for them to? You will always be you; they are not you. Make a wise decision and continue on your mission.

Don't feel pressured to complete everything at once. Certain projects need to be completed quickly. There are also a lot of assignments that, even if completed tomorrow, will yield no returns. Recognize that tomorrow will bring an equally overwhelming amount of work, and that's okay. When you get to some things, you will get to them. This isn't an excuse to be lazy; rather, it's meant to help you appreciate life and realize that nothing terrible will happen if you don't get dressed today.

A day comprises infinite hours, and time is a very valuable resource. I used to wear a watch at all times of the day to make sure I knew what time it was and could plan my best course of action. I only wear a watch to work now that I'm a moderate, partly because it's essential to what I do. I handicapped most tickers around me and tried not to worry too much about the time. I would like you to try this methodology for a short while. Some people who are generally pressed for time or anxious about the next thing find it irritating.

In my case, I try to immerse myself in whatever I am working on now. You'll think that time passes quickly during these "lost at the time" moments. These are normally going to be the most amazing moments of daily life. Schedule time to experience these times.

Reduce Your Thoughts

It would not be difficult to sense that our suspicions differ when we use a restricted thinking strategy. Remembering why we were so interested in moderation in the first place can help us understand that restricting our thinking entails focusing just on the important issues and putting the rest of the issues aside.

Not only that but maintaining this lifestyle suggests you are more likely because you have no other means of keeping yourself occupied and distracted from your worries. When you are no longer constantly acquiring clothing for your expanding closet, you will be able to identify the true motivator behind your consistent shopping: a fear of not being accepted and needed by others.

Without the need for haste, you now need to address the problem directly so that you may release the pressure this sensation is putting on you or perhaps identify trigger situations you can avoid.

It helps you distinguish between important and unnecessary, relieving strain because you can finally enjoy what you truly need to. Instead of becoming a prisoner to assets and the stresses that come with them, you may truly concentrate on the things that bring you excellence and tailor your life to your beliefs and perspective.

The entire experience also includes an incredible self-discovery component. It means you may focus more on who you are, what you truly value, and what you don't, even though you might be giving up certain possessions or bad habits you've adopted. When you finally identify what truly matters to you and live according to your internal clock, you can finally take a good, hard look at your life without the disruptive disruptions of a disorganized way of living or growing financial difficulties.

This gives you a more solid identity, which can instill confidence and help ease some of the anxiety that certain people may experience in social situations.

In this manner, you can be sure that your installments will always be processed on time and that you will always be aware of them beforehand.

Create an itinerary for yourself if you find yourself overburdened with family errands. I know it feels like you are raising a child, but trust me when I say daily and weekly by creating a task graph. By doing this, you'll cut down on unnecessary cleaning time and help you organize your calendar.

When it comes down to it, cleaning can absorb a lot of blame. Maybe those pricey precious stone candlesticks were expensive, or maybe your grandmother gave you a coat you detested but kept because you love her, and she is your grandmother.

In the end, separating one's emotions from the article is the most difficult thing to do in this kind of existence. No matter what we do with it, the memories associated with it will always be with us. Memories occur not because of the article itself but because we reflect on them while singing along in our hearts.

www.ingramcontent.com/pod-product-compliance
Lightning Source LLC
Chambersburg PA
CBHW052138110526
44591CB00012B/1773